C000133391

Transformed by the
HOLY SPIRIT

CWR

Copyright © Liz Babbs 2014

Published 2015 by CWR, Waverley Abbey House, Waverley Lane, Farnham, Surrey GU9 8EP, UK.
Registered Charity No. 294387. Registered Limited Company No. 1990308.

The right of Liz Babbs to be identified as the author of this work has been asserted by her in accordance
with the Copyright, Designs and Patents Act 1988, sections 77 and 78.

All rights reserved. No part of this publication may be reproduced, stored in a retrieval system, or
transmitted, in any form or by any means, electronic, mechanical, photocopying, recording or otherwise,
without the prior permission in writing of CWR.

For list of National Distributors visit www.cwr.org.uk/distributors

Unless otherwise indicated, all Scripture references are from the Holy Bible: New International Version
(Anglicised edition) copyright © 1979, 1984, 2011 by Biblica (formerly International Bible Society).
Used by permission of Hodder & Stoughton Publishers, an Hachette UK company. All rights reserved.
'NIV' is a registered trademark of Biblica. UK trademark number 1448790.

Other quotations are marked: Amplified: Scripture taken from the Amplified® Bible. copyright © 1954,
1958, 1962, 1964, 1965, 1987 by The Lockman Foundation. Used by permission. NASB: Scripture taken
from the NEW AMERICAN STANDARD BIBLE®, Copyright © 1960, 1962, 1963, 1968, 1971, 1972, 1973,
1975, 1977, 1995 by The Lockman Foundation. Used by permission. NCV: Scripture taken from the New
Century Version®. Copyright © 2005 by Thomas Nelson, Inc. Used by permission. All rights reserved.
NKJV: Scripture taken from the New King James Version®. Copyright © 1982 by Thomas Nelson. Used
by permission. All rights reserved. NLT: Scripture quotations marked NLT are taken from the Holy
Bible, New Living Translation, copyright © 1996, 2004, 2007, 2013. Used by permission of Tyndale
House Publishers, Inc., Wheaton, Illinois 60188. All rights reserved. *The Message*: Scripture taken from
The Message. Copyright © 1993, 1994, 1995, 1996, 2000, 2001, 2002. Used by permission of NavPress
Publishing Group.

Concept development, editing, design and production by CWR

Cover image: Istock/-M-I-S-H-A-

Printed in the UK by Page Bros.

ISBN: 978-1-78259-275-4

Every effort has been made to ensure that this book contains the correct permissions and references,
but if anything has been inadvertently overlooked the Publisher will be pleased to make the necessary
arrangements at the first opportunity. Please contact the Publisher directly.

Contents

Introduction

> The Spirit of God, who raised Jesus from the dead, lives in you. And just as God raised Christ Jesus from the dead, he will give life to your mortal bodies by this same Spirit living within you.
> (Rom. 8:11, NLT)

There is much misunderstanding and confusion about the Holy Spirit. It's the one member of the Trinity we hardly discuss and who in some churches is hidden in a dusty box in the corner marked: 'Handle with care – you could lose your congregation'! Hiding or suppressing the Holy Spirit makes little sense especially when the book of Acts celebrates the birth and spread of the Church through the Holy Spirit. The Holy Spirit is the power of God at work and without the Spirit – we, the Church, wouldn't exist!

The activity of the Holy Spirit has historically been a controversial topic of conversation. It is the more 'messy' member of the Trinity and can really challenge our thinking. But that does not mean we should avoid discussion, but rather clarify our thoughts and experiences in the light of Scripture to lay aside any myths, misunderstandings or hurt feelings. It's a clever tactic of the devil to cause confusion and suppress conversation, but then the devil lurks in dark shadows, whereas the Holy Spirit is the 'Spirit of truth' (John 16:13).

Many churches focus on God's Word while others focus on experiencing the Holy Spirit. As leading theologians John Stott and RT Kendall point out – the fullness lies in the Word and the Spirit. Scripture was inspired by and is illuminated by the Holy Spirit. You can't separate the Bible from the Spirit! Jesus overcame the lies of the devil in the wilderness through the power of the Word and the Holy Spirit.

Understanding the triune, three-in-one nature of God as Father, Son and Holy Spirit is essential. Christianity is not a pick 'n' mix spirituality or a multiple-choice questionnaire where you select one or two options out of three. You can't have the two (Father and Son) without the three, because God is three in one.

The Holy Spirit *is* the Spirit of God. To minimise the Holy Spirit is to minimise the power of God.

As I was standing on a London underground platform I sensed God give me a simple picture of the Trinity. The yellow line, parallel to the platform edge, was God, the white line marking the platform edge was Jesus, but the train was the Holy Spirit – as we get on board our faith takes off! The Holy Spirit is like the touch paper activating our faith and causing it to ignite. The Greek word *Dunamis*, from which we get our word dynamite, is the same word Jesus used when He said to His disciples, 'But you will receive power when the Holy Spirit comes on you; and you will be my witnesses in Jerusalem, and in all Judea and Samaria, and to the ends of the earth' (Acts 1:8). In effect, Jesus was saying, 'You will receive explosive power like dynamite when the Holy Spirit comes upon you, empowering you to share me with others.'

The words on that underground platform between the yellow and white lines were also a timely reminder: 'Mind the gap.' Many are not living an 'ignited' faith because of a gap in their understanding of the Person and activity of the Holy Spirit. To ignore the Holy Spirit is to miss out on the 'dynamite' fuelling mission, growth and transformation.

As a friend of mine says, 'There's a war on the truth', and she is right. To ignore the Holy Spirit, the resurrection power of Jesus, is to go into battle unprepared and vulnerable without the full supernatural armoury and weaponry needed. It is the Holy Spirit, the Revealer of truth, who equips, guides and empowers us to do *'great exploits'* in Jesus' name (Dan. 11:32, NKJV). When you read the whole Bible through the lens of the Holy Spirit, it is revolutionary.

During the period I trialled the material for this book with my group, I saw a new authority and boldness emerge as individuals became empowered through their growing knowledge of the Holy Spirit. We debated the hard questions, discussed faulty teaching and clarified our thoughts on the Spirit in the light of God's Word. Our journey across six weeks was transformational. My prayer, as you study *Transformed by the Holy Spirit*, is that you too will grow in authority as you learn more about the Holy Spirit.

The aim of this book is not to define the Holy Spirit, but to provide a biblical framework allowing you to grow in awareness and understanding of the Holy Spirit as you reflect on key passages of Scripture in the Old and New Testaments. Many of these passages (like creation, Jesus tested in the wilderness, Pentecost and Saul/Paul's conversion experience) will be very familiar to you, and others, ie Revelation, might be less familiar. But as you study all six studies you will see how one passage illuminates another and gain fresh revelation and a deeper understanding of God. 'For the word of God is alive and active. Sharper than any double-edged sword' (Heb. 4:12).

In addition to the more traditional Bible study approach with group discussion questions etc, I have woven into these studies the opportunity for personal and group reflection and meditation. Before the first study's Session Focus and at the end of the following five studies, I also invite you to deepen your experience through listening to an imaginative meditation where you step inside a scene related to the Bible passage. I have seen God work very powerfully through these meditations across the years.

The following prayer, inspired by the Holy Spirit on Pentecost Sunday, was written on Eastbourne Pier as I watched the sun set.

Holy Spirit
Pentecost fire
Fuel my desire
To know You.
Fan into flames
The embers of my faith
And give me a taste
Of heaven on earth;
A glorious rebirth
A renewed vision
So all my decisions
Are earthed in You.
© Liz Babbs

Created by
the Holy Spirit
Genesis 1:1–31

Thought Starter

Describe how to make a cup of tea starting with the words 'In the beginning'. One member of the group begins with their sentence then each member contributes a sentence until the task is complete.

Alternatively, if you're studying this book independently, write the stages of making a cup of tea as a series of sentences in a journal.

Opening Prayer

Lord of all creation, increase our awareness and understanding of the Holy Spirit as we study Your Word. Amen.

Bible Readings

Hebrews 11:3

By faith we understand that the universe was formed at God's command, so that what is seen was not made out of what was visible.

Psalm 104:30

When you send your Spirit,
they are created,
and you renew the face of the ground.

John 1:1–3 (Amplified)

In the beginning [before all time] was the Word (Christ), and the Word was with God, and the Word was God Himself.
He was present originally with God.
All things were made *and* came into existence through Him; and without Him was not even one thing made that has come into being.

Job 33:4

The Spirit of God has made me;
the breath of the Almighty gives me life.

Acts 17:24-25

> The God who made the world and everything in it is the
> Lord of heaven and earth and does not live in temples
> built by human hands. And he is not served by human
> hands, as if he needed anything. Rather, he himself gives
> everyone life and breath and everything else.

Eye Opener

I write books on my tablet and sometimes the autocorrect
gets carried away with itself; even creating it's own
translation of the Bible. For example, the title of my
book was autocorrected to 'Transformed by the Holy
Sprout'! And when I was writing this study on Genesis
the autocorrect had the Spirit of God 'hoovering' over the
waters. Now although that's a useful work of the Spirit,
it does not make a lot of sense, even if it does add new
meaning to 'For you are dust, And to dust you shall return'
(Gen. 3:19, NASB).

My tablet is not Christian and neither was it created directly
by God. It was made by a multinational corporation. Its DNA
is not God's, like ours. We were created by God, for God, in
our Maker's image.

Setting the Scene

Genesis means 'beginning' or 'origin' and Moses is thought
to be the author. This theological narrative sets the stage,
introducing most of the major doctrines that are later
developed in the rest of the Bible.

It's amazing to think that before God spoke nothing existed!
That's the power of God's words. God spoke everything
into being through the Holy Spirit and we are the prized
possessions of that creative process – God's masterpiece made
uniquely for intimacy with Him. All three members of the
Trinity were involved in creation and we are made in their
image: 'Then God said, "Let us make mankind in our image,
in our likeness"' (Gen. 1:26).

The Hebrew word for spirit, *Ruach* (translated as 'breath' or 'wind'), appears first in Genesis 1:2 as 'the Spirit of God', which was 'hovering over the waters'. It is the same word used in Psalm 33:6: 'By the word of the LORD the heavens were made, their starry host by the breath of his mouth.' The word 'hovering' is an intimate picture of God's nurturing care of creation and is the same word used in Deuteronomy 32:11 to describe an eagle hovering over its nest. That same 'hovering' of the Holy Spirit was over Mary, and resulted in the greatest miracle of all – the conception of Jesus: 'The angel answered, "The Holy Spirit will come on you, and the power of the Most High will overshadow you"' (Luke 1:35).

Imaginative Meditation

In preparation for the Session Focus it would be helpful to watch the video 'Spirit of Creation' on my YouTube channel. The audio version is also available as track one, *Created by the Holy Spirit*, of the CD *Transformed by the Holy Spirit*. Available from **www.lizbabbs.com**

The short video combines visuals of creation with Scripture and poetry; highlighting the presence of the Holy Spirit from the very beginning of existence.

Session Focus

Relax, close your eyes and imagine yourself sitting in a reclining cinema seat with a 360-degree 3D interactive screen around you.

As you listen to this passage of Scripture read to you, see if any words or sentences become highlighted for you in some way or if any images stay lodged on the cinema screen of your mind. At the end of the reading, spend a couple of minutes in silence asking God to show you what He might be saying to you through any words, thoughts or images that drop into your mind. Then discuss your thoughts with your group.

Alternatively, if you are studying this book independently, why not listen to the passage using a Bible audio recording and write your thoughts down in a journal.

The Beginning (Gen. 1:1–31)

In the beginning God created the heavens and the earth. Now the earth was formless and empty, darkness was over the surface of the deep, and the Spirit of God was hovering over the waters.

And God said, 'Let there be light,' and there was light. God saw that the light was good, and he separated the light from the darkness. God called the light 'day', and the darkness he called 'night'. And there was evening, and there was morning – the first day.

And God said, 'Let there be a vault between the waters to separate water from water.' So God made the vault and separated the water under the vault from the water above it. And it was so. God called the vault 'sky'. And there was evening, and there was morning – the second day.

And God said, 'Let the water under the sky be gathered to one place, and let dry ground appear.' And it was so. God called the dry ground 'land', and the gathered waters he called 'seas'. And God saw that it was good.

Then God said, 'Let the land produce vegetation: seed-bearing plants and trees on the land that bear fruit with seed in it, according to their various kinds.' And it was so. The land produced vegetation: plants bearing seed according to their kinds and trees bearing fruit with seed in it according to their kinds. And God saw that it was good. And there was evening, and there was morning – the third day.

And God said, 'Let there be lights in the vault of the sky to separate the day from the night, and let them serve as signs to mark sacred times, and days and years, and let them be lights in the vault of the sky to give light on the earth.' And it was so. God made two great lights – the greater light to govern the day and the lesser light to govern the night. He also made the stars. God set them in the vault of the sky to give light on the earth, to govern the day and the night,

and to separate light from darkness. And God saw that it was good. And there was evening, and there was morning – the fourth day.

And God said, 'Let the water teem with living creatures, and let birds fly above the earth across the vault of the sky.' So God created the great creatures of the sea and every living thing with which the water teems and that moves about in it, according to their kinds, and every winged bird according to its kind. And God saw that it was good. God blessed them and said, 'Be fruitful and increase in number and fill the water in the seas, and let the birds increase on the earth.' And there was evening, and there was morning – the fifth day.

And God said, 'Let the land produce living creatures according to their kinds: the livestock, the creatures that move along the ground, and the wild animals, each according to its kind.' And it was so. God made the wild animals according to their kinds, the livestock according to their kinds, and all the creatures that move along the ground according to their kinds. And God saw that it was good.

Then God said, 'Let us make mankind in our image, in our likeness, so that they may rule over the fish in the sea and the birds in the sky, over the livestock and all the wild animals, and over all the creatures that move along the ground.'

So God created mankind in his own image,
in the image of God he created them;
male and female he created them.

God blessed them and said to them, 'Be fruitful and increase in number; fill the earth and subdue it. Rule over the fish in the sea and the birds in the sky and over every living creature that moves on the ground.'

Then God said, 'I give you every seed-bearing plant on the face of the whole earth and every tree that has fruit with seed in it. They will be yours for food. And to all the beasts of the earth and all the birds in the sky and all the creatures that move along the ground – everything that has the breath of life in it – I give every green plant for food.' And it was so.

God saw all that he had made, and it was very good. And there was evening, and there was morning – the sixth day.

Discussion Starters

1. What are your thoughts on creation?

_____
_____
_____
_____
_____

2. Where do you see the Holy Spirit in the creation story?

_____
_____
_____
_____
_____

3. What is revealed about God in this passage?

_____
_____
_____
_____
_____

4. What is revealed about mankind?

_____
_____
_____
_____
_____

5. Is the Bible account of creation compatible with the theory of evolution?

_____
_____
_____
_____
_____

6. Why did God create life in the order that He did?

_____

_____

_____

_____

_____

7. What might have happened if God hadn't created the world?

_____

_____

_____

_____

_____

8. What might the Holy Spirit be saying to you about how to look after God's creation today?

_____

_____

_____

_____

_____

Final Thoughts

Genesis answers three of the fundamental questions people generally ask: Who am I? Why am I here? Where am I heading?

The first chapter of Genesis emphasises that God is Master of creation. God was ... God is ... and will always be ... God. He doesn't say anything without meaning. His very breath reveals His creative power and almighty presence. And the Spirit of God is the power of God at work creating the world.

I've sometimes wondered why God didn't create everything in one go. Was He laying down a pattern of work and rest, demonstrating the need for defined periods of time with boundaries, or simply showing the rhythm of nature? I love the fact that God rested on the seventh 'day' (be that literal or poetic) so He could enjoy His own handiwork. When was the last time you stood back to enjoy something in your life?

Closing Prayer

Father Almighty, Maker and Creator, every word You spoke had meaning and creative potential. Help us to use our words creatively and not destructively. Amen.

Space to Journal

_____

_____

_____

_____

_____

_____

_____

_____

_____

_____

_____

_____

_____

_____

_____

_____

_____

_____

_____

_____

_____

_____

_____

_____

_____

_____

_____

_____

_____

Equipped by
the Holy Spirit
Exodus 31:1–11

Thought Starter

Share your hobbies or creative interests with the group or journal them if you're studying independently.

Opening Prayer

Creator Father, increase our awareness of the gifting You have placed in us and help us to use those gifts in the service and expansion of Your kingdom. Amen.

Bible Readings

Genesis 1:1
In the beginning God created

2 Timothy 1:6
For this reason I remind you to fan into flame the gift of God, which is in you through the laying on of my hands.

Romans 11:29 (Amplified)
For God's gifts and His call are irrevocable. [He never withdraws them when once they are given, and He does not change His mind about those to whom He gives His grace or to whom He sends His call.]

Acts 17:28
'For in him we live and move and have our being.' As some of your own poets have said, 'We are his offspring.'

Psalm 104:30 (NLT)
When you give them your breath, life is created, and you renew the face of the earth.

Exodus 20:1–3
And God spoke all these words:
'I am the LORD your God, who brought you out of Egypt, out of the land of slavery.
'You shall have no other gods before me.'

2 Corinthians 3:17
Now the Lord is the Spirit, and where the Spirit of the Lord is, there is freedom.

Eye Opener

The first five words of the Bible tell us that God created, 'In the beginning God created' (Gen. 1:1), so it shouldn't be any surprise that God is the Author of creativity, but sometimes we don't make that connection.

As a young person I was described by one of my parents as being a 'Jack of all trades, master of none'. I received this comment negatively as it seemed to suggest I wasn't good at anything. I carried that label into my adult life and it hampered my creativity for many years.

As an author I produce a variety of non-fiction books, gift books and CDs. So does that 'variety' mean I'm not gifted as an author and that none of my publications are any good? Fortunately, the sales of my publications and feedback suggest otherwise. I'm also a performance artist, performing poetry and meditations classically in concert. I have my own one-woman comedy show too. Does performing comedy negate my gifting as a spiritual director creating meditative material and writing Bible study books like this one? No! We tend to compartmentalise creativity but God does not. God is multi-creative and as we're made in His image, we're multi-creative too.

Many of us carry unhelpful labels from authority figures, teachers or parents that can cripple our creative and artistic ability. God has given us gifts and skills. We are gifted. That's not bragging; it's fact!

Setting the Scene

In the Old Testament, the Holy Spirit was given to people to fulfil a particular task. It was not until the resurrection of Jesus and the coming of the Holy Spirit in Acts 2 that people were permanently filled with the Spirit.

Here at the beginning of Exodus 31, God has selected the most gifted artist and master craftsman Bezalel for a specific task. God supercharged him with the Holy Spirit so he has everything he needs to complete the building of the tabernacle, according to God's instructions. It's interesting that artists were the first people recorded in the Bible to be equiped by the Holy Spirit. Bezalel is the supervising artist, but God also gave him an assistant called Oholiab and supplied him with an artistic support team who were divinely gifted to create the works of art and sacred furniture. All these artists and craftspeople were already gifted, but had their skills enhanced by God through the Holy Spirit. What an awesome assignment – to build the house of God!

Session Focus

Relax, close your eyes and imagine yourself as one of the artists appointed by God to build the tabernacle to house the presence of God.

As you listen to this passage of Scripture read to you, see if any words or sentences stand out or become highlighted for you in some way. At the end of the reading, spend a couple of minutes in silence asking God to show you what He might be saying to you through any words, thoughts or images that drop into your mind. Then discuss your thoughts with your group.

Alternatively, if you are studying this book independently, why not listen to the passage using a Bible audio recording and write your thoughts down in a journal.

Bezalel and Oholiab (Exod. 31:1–11)

Then the LORD said to Moses, 'See I have chosen Bezalel son of Uri, the son of Hur, of the tribe of Judah, and I have filled him with the Spirit of God, with wisdom, with understanding, with knowledge and with all kinds of skills – to make artistic designs for work in gold, silver and bronze, to cut and set stones, to work in wood, and to engage in all kinds of crafts. Moreover, I have appointed Oholiab son of Ahisamak, of the tribe of Dan, to help him. Also I have given ability to all the skilled workers to make everything I have commanded you: the tent of meeting, the ark of the covenant law with the atonement cover on it, and all the other furnishings of the tent – the table and its articles, the pure gold lampstand and all its accessories, the altar of incense, the altar of burnt offering and

all its utensils, the basin with its stand – and also the woven garments, both the sacred garments for Aaron the priest and the garments for his sons when they serve as priests, and the anointing oil and fragrant incense for the Holy Place. They are to make them just as I commanded you.'

Discussion Starters

1. Why was Bezalel chosen for this task?

_____
_____
_____
_____
_____

2. What is the significance of Bezalel and Oholiab being from different tribes?

_____
_____
_____
_____
_____

3. How might you have responded if God had asked you to make a sacred object for His tabernacle? How do you respond now if God asks you to do something?

_____
_____
_____
_____
_____

4. What is the difference between our natural gifts and spiritual gifts?

_____

_____

_____

_____

_____

5. Are gifts simply abilities you haven't recognised or had confirmed?

_____

_____

_____

_____

_____

6. What has helped you recognise your creative gifts?

_____

_____

_____

_____

_____

7. How does the Holy Spirit enhance our gifts?

_____

_____

_____

_____

_____

8. How does God inspire you?

_____

_____

_____

_____

_____

Final Thoughts

As we see from this passage, the artists were the first people referred to in the Bible who were filled with the Holy Spirit and it was for a purpose and to accomplish a task. The Holy Spirit gives people the ability to create. And when you partner with the triune God, you can't go wrong. Bezalel was the instrument chosen by God to lead this task and he responded with obedience. The tabernacle was a divine–human partnership that left no room for error. God had a plan with a precise order, like creation, and there was no room for discussion. God chose men and women to create the sacred works of art (Exod. 35:25–29), which had already been described in detail to Moses. There was no room for creative licence. The materials for the symbols of God's presence had to be the best and the workmanship, the finest. But all this was possible because God Himself enhanced their skills through the Holy Spirit.

Closing Prayer

Lord of all creativity, thank You for equipping us through our gifts and talents. Help us to flow in the fullness of that gifting through Your Holy Spirit. Amen.

Imaginative Meditation

The following imaginative meditation is voiced over music on track two, *Equipped by the Holy Spirit*, of the CD *Transformed by the Holy Spirit*. Available from **www.lizbabbs.com**

Imagine God has asked you to create something that will bless others, which could be art, craft, baking, poetry or music.

What is He asking you to make?

What materials do you need?

How do you feel about your assignment?

Now imagine God affirming your creative ability and then supercharging it through the Holy Spirit.

How do you feel now?

What do you do next?

> Praise the LORD.
> Praise God in his sanctuary;
> praise him in his mighty heavens.
> Praise him for his acts of power;
> praise him for his surpassing greatness.
> Praise him with the sounding of the trumpet,
> praise him with the harp and lyre,
> praise him with tambourine and dancing,
> praise him with the strings and pipe,
> praise him with the clash of cymbals,
> praise him with resounding cymbals.
> Let everything that has breath praise the LORD.
> (Psa. 150)

Space to Journal

_____
_____
_____
_____
_____
_____
_____
_____
_____
_____
_____
_____
_____
_____
_____
_____
_____
_____
_____
_____
_____
_____
_____
_____
_____
_____
_____
_____
_____
_____
_____
_____
_____
_____

Trained by the Holy Spirit
Luke 4:1–15

Thought Starter

Have you ever been tempted to take an extra chocolate from a box, or biscuit or cake from a plate without asking? Or, if you prefer savoury snacks, have you ever been tempted to take extra peanuts or crisps? Share your thoughts with the group or journal them if you're studying this independently.

Opening Prayer

Lord, reveal Your Word to us through the power of the Holy Spirit and deepen our understanding and awareness of the Holy Spirit's activity in our lives. Amen.

Bible Readings

Romans 8:26

In the same way, the Spirit helps us in our weakness. We do not know what we ought to pray for, but the Spirit himself intercedes for us through wordless groans.

1 Corinthians 10:13

No temptation has overtaken you except what is common to mankind. And God is faithful; he will not let you be tempted beyond what you can bear. But when you are tempted, he will also provide a way out so that you can endure it.

James 4:6 (Amplified)

But He gives us more and more grace (power of the Holy Spirit, to meet this evil tendency and all others fully). That is why He says, God sets Himself against the proud and haughty, but gives grace [continually] to the lowly (those who are humble enough to receive it).

1 Peter 5:8–9 (Amplified)

Be well balanced (temperate, sober of mind), be vigilant *and* cautious at all times; for that enemy of yours, the devil, roams around like a lion roaring [in fierce hunger], seeking someone to seize upon *and* devour.
Withstand him; be firm in faith [against his onset—rooted,

established, strong, immovable, and determined], knowing that the same (identical) sufferings are appointed to your brotherhood (the whole body of Christians) throughout the world.

Hebrews 4:12

For the word of God is alive and active. Sharper than any double-edged sword, it penetrates even to dividing soul and spirit, joints and marrow; it judges the thoughts and attitudes of the heart.

1 Corinthians 9:24–27 (NLT)

Don't you realize that in a race everyone runs, but only one person gets the prize? So run to win! All athletes are disciplined in their training. They do it to win a prize that will fade away, but we do it for an eternal prize. So I run with purpose in every step. I am not just shadowboxing. I discipline my body like an athlete, training it to do what it should. Otherwise, I fear that after preaching to others I myself might be disqualified.

1 Timothy 6:12 (NLT)

Fight the good fight for the true faith. Hold tightly to the eternal life to which God has called you, which you have declared so well before many witnesses.

Eye Opener

I must admit I once ate the bottom layer of a box of chocolates that was bought as a Christmas present for my dad's personal assistant. It was pure temptation and I gave in to it. I just needed that chocolate fix and could tell by the shape of the gift wrapped box that they were my favourite brand of chocolates. So I ate my way through the bottom layer and carefully rewrapped the box; placing it back under the Christmas tree. I'd like to say I was a child when this happened, but I was twenty years old! Fortunately, or unfortunately for me, my mother noticed the Christmas wrapping paper was torn and investigated further. As soon as she opened the wrapping and looked inside the box she was horrified, and immediately knew it was me. Boy, did I get in trouble, and what's more,

she's never let me forget it since! But there has been one bonus, she's bought me a box of my favourite chocolates for Christmas ever since.

Setting the Scene

> When all the people were being baptised, Jesus was baptised too. And as he was praying, heaven was opened and the Holy Spirit descended on him in bodily form like a dove. And a voice came from heaven: 'You are my Son, whom I love; with you I am well pleased.'
> (Luke 3:21–22)

It's interesting that straight after Jesus was baptised and His Father told Him how much He loved Him, He was 'sent' (some translations say 'driven') into the desert (Mark 1:12)! If it had been me I might have been tempted to say, 'Well thanks, Dad!' It seems like a harsh act for a loving Father, but this is 'tough love'. The desert was like boot camp – a training ground where the Holy Spirit would be like Jesus' personal trainer. In the desert, Jesus would go head to head with the devil and as a result of persistent temptation and extreme combat, Jesus would be fully equipped for ministry and ready to undertake His world-changing mission. Soldiers go through rigorous training in preparation for war, but Jesus' testing was beyond comprehension – He endured six long weeks' of extreme boot camp for the sake of humankind.

I work out at a gym, following an exercise programme devised by a personal trainer. I train with a friend and this keeps me accountable and means we both exercise even when we don't feel like it, which is most times! We help each other push through. After six weeks our trainer adjusts the level of difficulty of our programme: adding in new exercises and heavier weights. Our bodies soon get into their 'comfort zones' even when working out, so we regularly need challenging to work harder. The Holy Spirit is like a personal trainer working alongside us, training and equipping us so that our faith is strong enough to withstand anything the devil might hurl at us.

It is with this strength that we are enabled to say, like Jesus, '*Get behind Me, Satan!*' (Luke 4:8, Amplified).

Session Focus

Relax, close your eyes and imagine yourself in the desert with Jesus.

As you listen to this passage of Scripture read to you from two different translations, see if any words or sentences stand out or become highlighted for you in some way. At the end of the reading, spend a couple of minutes in silence; asking God to show you what He might be saying to you through any words, thoughts or images that drop into your mind. Then discuss your thoughts with your group.

Alternatively, if you are studying this book independently, why not listen to the passage using a Bible audio recording and write your thoughts down in a journal.

Jesus is Tested in the Wilderness (Luke 4:1–15)

Jesus, full of the Holy Spirit, left the Jordan and was led by the Spirit into the wilderness, where for forty days he was tempted by the devil. He ate nothing during those days, and at the end of them he was hungry.

The devil said to him, 'If you are the Son of God, tell this stone to become bread.'

Jesus answered, 'It is written: "Man shall not live on bread alone."'

The devil led him up to a high place and showed him in an instant all the kingdoms of the world. And he said to him, 'I will give you all their authority and splendour; it has been given to me, and I can give it to anyone I want to. If you worship me, it will all be yours.'

Jesus answered, 'It is written: "Worship the Lord your God and serve him only."'

The devil led him to Jerusalem and had him stand on the highest point of the temple. 'If you are the Son of God,' he said, 'throw yourself down from here. For it is written:

'"He will command his angels concerning you

to guard you carefully;
they will lift you up in their hands,
so that you will not strike your foot against a stone."'
Jesus answered, 'It is said: "Do not put the Lord your God
to the test."'
When the devil had finished all this tempting, he left him
until an opportune time.
Jesus returned to Galilee in the power of the Spirit, and
news about him spread through the whole countryside. He was
teaching in their synagogues, and everyone praised him.

Tested by the Devil (Luke 4:1–15, *The Message*)

Now Jesus, full of the Holy Spirit, left the Jordan and was
led by the Spirit into the wild. For forty wilderness days and
nights he was tested by the Devil. He ate nothing during those
days, and when the time was up he was hungry.

The Devil, playing on his hunger, gave the first test:
'Since you're God's Son, command this stone to turn into
a loaf of bread.'

Jesus answered by quoting Deuteronomy: 'It takes more
than bread to really live.'

For the second test he led him up and spread out all the
kingdoms of the earth on display at once. Then the Devil said,
'They're yours in all their splendor to serve your pleasure. I'm in
charge of them all and can turn them over to whomever I wish.
Worship me and they're yours, the whole works.'

Jesus refused, again backing his refusal with Deuteronomy:
'Worship the Lord your God and only the Lord your God.
Serve him with absolute single-heartedness.'

For the third test the Devil took him to Jerusalem and
put him on top of the Temple. He said, 'If you are God's Son,
jump. It's written, isn't it, that "he has placed you in the care of
angels to protect you; they will catch you; you won't so much
as stub your toe on a stone"?'

'Yes,' said Jesus, 'and it's also written, "Don't you dare tempt
the Lord your God."'

That completed the testing. The Devil retreated temporarily,
lying in wait for another opportunity.

Jesus returned to Galilee powerful in the Spirit. News that he was back spread through the countryside. He taught in their meeting places to everyone's acclaim and pleasure.

Discussion Starters

1. How does this passage link up with creation and the Garden of Eden?

_____

_____

_____

_____

_____

2. What are the three temptations of Jesus?

_____

_____

_____

_____

_____

3. What is the progression in the way Satan tempts Jesus?

_____

_____

_____

_____

_____

4. How does Jesus counter the devil?

_____

_____

_____

_____

_____

5. In what ways does the devil try to attack you?

_____

_____

_____

_____

_____

6. How do you counter the devil?

_____

_____

_____

_____

_____

7. What is the significance of the devil saying 'if you are the Son of God'?

_____

_____

_____

_____

_____

8. How do we know when we're hearing from God and not the devil?

_____

_____

_____

_____

_____

Final Thoughts

We often wish the Christian road were easier, with no obstacles thrown in our pathway, but the truth is we need those challenges to sharpen our faith and build our spiritual muscles. There's a saying, 'What doesn't kill you makes you stronger', and that's true in many ways.

After Jesus was tested in the wilderness, He returned to Galilee 'full of' the Holy Spirit (Luke 4:14, Amplified) and 'powerful in the Spirit' (Luke 4:14, *The Message*). Our trials strengthen us. When life gets easier we have a tendency to become lazy and our faith can weaken as a result.

There is no escape from temptation and trials in our lives. Jesus didn't escape them and neither do we. As the Messiah, Jesus didn't use His super powers like Superman to defeat the enemy, He quoted Scripture, the truth, to combat the enemy's lies. Scripture is the 'sword of the Spirit' (Eph. 6:17), our ultimate offensive weapon, lie annihilator and truth tester.

Closing Prayer

Lord, help us to stand firm against the enemy's lies and to wield the sword of the Spirit, in Jesus' name. Amen.

Imaginative Meditation

The following imaginative meditation is voiced over music on track three, *Trained by the Holy Spirit*, of the CD *Transformed by the Holy Spirit*. Available from **www.lizbabbs.com**

Imagine yourself trapped in a hot barren landscape without food and water.

What can you see?

What can you hear?

How do you feel?

What do you need most?

Now imagine a harsh authority figure standing over you, accusing you of something you've done wrong. This person says you're a failure; a worthless nobody who'll never amount to anything.

How do you feel?

Now imagine yourself wielding a heavy sword, which is the sword of the Spirit, and facing your accuser, declaring, 'I am a beloved child of God whose identity is in Jesus Christ. Get out of my way, in Jesus' name.'

Space to Journal

_____
_____
_____
_____
_____
_____
_____
_____
_____
_____
_____
_____
_____
_____
_____
_____
_____
_____
_____
_____
_____

Thought Starter

Have you or someone you know ever tried to speak another language and found yourself saying the wrong word by mistake? Discuss with the group or journal your thoughts if you're studying this book independently.

Opening Prayer

Lord, thank You for the gift of Your Holy Spirit. Still our minds and open Scripture to us so that we might learn more about the Spirit of God. Amen.

Bible Readings

The Festival of Weeks – Deuteronomy 16:9–10

Count seven weeks from the time you begin to put the sickle to the standing corn. Then celebrate the Festival of Weeks to the LORD your God by giving a freewill offering in proportion to the blessings the LORD your God has given you.

Ezekiel 37:13–14

Then you, my people, will know that I am the LORD, when I open your graves and bring you up from them. I will put my Spirit in you and you will live, and I will settle you in your own land. Then you will know that I the LORD have spoken, and I have done it, declares the LORD.

The Promise of the Holy Spirit – John 7:37–39 (NKJV)

On the last day, that great *day* of the feast, Jesus stood and cried out, saying, 'If anyone thirsts, let him come to Me and drink. He who believes in Me, as the Scripture has said, out of his heart will flow rivers of living water.' But this He spoke concerning the Spirit, whom those believing in Him would receive; for the Holy Spirit was not yet *given*, because Jesus was not yet glorified.

Romans 8:9

You, however, are not in the realm of the flesh but are in the realm of the Spirit, if indeed the Spirit of God lives

Empowered by
the Holy Spirit
Acts 2:1–41

in you. And if anyone does not have the Spirit of Christ, they do not belong to Christ.

Romans 8:11 (NLT)

The Spirit of God, who raised Jesus from the dead, lives in you. And just as God raised Christ Jesus from the dead, he will give life to your mortal bodies by this same Spirit living within you.

Luke 11:11-13

Which of you fathers, if your son asks for a fish, will give him a snake instead? Or if he asks for an egg, will give him a scorpion? If you then, though you are evil, know how to give good gifts to your children, how much more will your Father in heaven give the Holy Spirit to those who ask him!

Acts 4:31

After they prayed, the place where they were meeting was shaken. And they were all filled with the Holy Spirit and spoke the word of God boldly.

Galatians 5:16 (NLT)

So I say, let the Holy Spirit guide your lives. Then you won't be doing what your sinful nature craves.

Galatians 5:25 (NLT)

Since we are living by the Spirit, let us follow the Spirit's leading in every part of our lives.

Eye Opener

Although I'm British and speak English, I'm sometimes misunderstood in America and what's more, I misunderstand things there too. There have been some very funny incidents. One time was when I was at an American TV studio and about to be interviewed live on Christian television. When I arrived at the studio, I was given a tour and the 'rest room' was pointed out to me. I remember thinking what wonderful provision this was and imagined myself reclining on the sofa, relaxing and drinking refreshments before my interview. What a shock I had when I entered the rest room and realised it was the toilets! I still can't work out why Americans use the term rest room, as this is not my idea of rest!

Setting the Scene

While the Gospel of Luke outlines the ministry of Jesus on earth until He was taken up into heaven, the book of Acts, the second book written by Luke, focuses on the disciples and the growth of the Early Church. Jesus' ministry on earth was followed by His ministry from heaven exercised by the Holy Spirit through His disciples.

In the first chapter of Acts we see the disciples praying and waiting expectantly for many days in an upper room in Jerusalem. They were doing exactly what Jesus had instructed – waiting for the gift of the Holy Spirit:

> Do not leave Jerusalem, but wait for the gift my Father promised, which you have heard me speak about. For John baptised with water, but in a few days you will be baptised with the Holy Spirit ... you will receive power when the Holy Spirit comes on you; and you will be my witnesses in Jerusalem, and in all Judea and Samaria, and to the ends of the earth.
> (Acts 1:4–5,8)

Jesus is explaining that even though He had to ascend to His Father, His presence would remain with the disciples through the Holy Spirit. I summed this up poetically as – the Son had to go so the Spirit could come 'n' flow! And just as the Spirit descended on Jesus, equipping Him for ministry, so the Spirit equips us too.

Pentecost comes from a Greek word meaning fifty and was a Jewish festival, the Festival of Weeks, celebrating fifty days after Passover (Deut. 16:16). Jesus was crucified at Passover but ascended forty days later. The Holy Spirit came in power fifty days after Jesus' resurrection – ten days after the ascension.

The Holy Spirit coming at Pentecost is like a spectacular scene from a Hollywood movie – thunderous wind breaking into tongues of fire, which rest on the disciples. This outward sign of the presence and power of the Holy Spirit is dramatic to say the least, but also fulfils John the Baptist's words:

'I baptise you with water. But one who is more powerful than I will come, the straps of whose sandals I am not worthy to untie. He will baptise you with the Holy Spirit and fire' (Luke 3:16). Fire is a symbol of the power and presence of the Holy Spirit. At Mount Sinai, fire came down from heaven confirming God's law (Exod. 19:16–18), at Pentecost it rests on each believer, symbolising an anointing and being set apart for a purpose.

Session Focus

Relax, close your eyes and imagine yourself as one of the crowd hearing about the Holy Spirit.

As you listen to this passage of Scripture read to you, see if any words or sentences stand out or become highlighted for you in some way. At the end of the reading, spend a couple of minutes in silence; asking God to show you what He might be saying to you through any words, thoughts or images that drop into your mind. Then discuss your thoughts with your group.

Alternatively, if you are studying this book independently, why not listen to the passage using a Bible audio recording and write your thoughts down in a journal.

The Holy Spirit Comes at Pentecost (Acts 2:1–41, NLT)

On the day of Pentecost all the believers were meeting together in one place. Suddenly, there was a sound from heaven like the roaring of a mighty windstorm, and it filled the house where they were sitting. Then, what looked like flames or tongues of fire appeared and settled on each of them. And everyone present was filled with the Holy Spirit and began speaking in other languages, as the Holy Spirit gave them this ability.

At that time there were devout Jews from every nation living in Jerusalem. When they heard the loud noise, everyone came running, and they were bewildered to hear their own languages being spoken by the believers.

They were completely amazed. 'How can this be?' they exclaimed. 'These people are all from Galilee, and yet we hear them speaking in our own native languages! Here we are—

Parthians, Medes, Elamites, people from Mesopotamia, Judea, Cappadocia, Pontus, the province of Asia, Phrygia, Pamphylia, Egypt, and the areas of Libya around Cyrene, visitors from Rome (both Jews and converts to Judaism), Cretans, and Arabs. And we all hear these people speaking in our own languages about the wonderful things God has done!' They stood there amazed and perplexed. 'What can this mean?' they asked each other.

But others in the crowd ridiculed them, saying, 'They're just drunk, that's all!'

Then Peter stepped forward with the eleven other apostles and shouted to the crowd, 'Listen carefully, all of you, fellow Jews and residents of Jerusalem! Make no mistake about this. These people are not drunk, as some of you are assuming. Nine o'clock in the morning is much too early for that. No, what you see was predicted long ago by the prophet Joel:

"In the last days," God says, "I will pour out my Spirit upon all people. Your sons and daughters will prophesy. Your young men will see visions, and your old men will dream dreams.

In those days I will pour out my Spirit even on my servants—men and women alike—and they will prophesy.

And I will cause wonders in the heavens above and signs on the earth below—blood and fire and clouds of smoke.

The sun will become dark, and the moon will turn blood red before that great and glorious day of the LORD arrives.

But everyone who calls on the name of the LORD will be saved."

'People of Israel, listen! God publicly endorsed Jesus the Nazarene by doing powerful miracles, wonders, and signs through him, as you well know. But God knew what would happen, and his prearranged plan was carried out when Jesus was betrayed. With the help of lawless Gentiles, you nailed him to a cross and killed him. But God released him from the horrors of death and raised him back to life, for death could not keep him in its grip. King David said this about him:

"I see that the LORD is always with me. I will not be shaken, for he is right beside me.

No wonder my heart is glad, and my tongue shouts his praises! My body rests in hope.

For you will not leave my soul among the dead or allow your Holy One to rot in the grave.

You have shown me the way of life, and you will fill me with the joy of your presence."

'Dear brothers, think about this! You can be sure that the patriarch David wasn't referring to himself, for he died and was buried, and his tomb is still here among us. But he was a prophet, and he knew God had promised with an oath that one of David's own descendants would sit on his throne. David was looking into the future and speaking of the Messiah's resurrection. He was saying that God would not leave him among the dead or allow his body to rot in the grave.

'God raised Jesus from the dead, and we are all witnesses of this. Now he is exalted to the place of highest honor in heaven, at God's right hand. And the Father, as he had promised, gave him the Holy Spirit to pour out upon us, just as you see and hear today. For David himself never ascended into heaven, yet he said,

"The LORD said to my Lord, 'Sit in the place of honor at my right hand until I humble your enemies, making them a footstool under your feet.'"

'So let everyone in Israel know for certain that God has made this Jesus, whom you crucified, to be both Lord and Messiah!'

Peter's words pierced their hearts, and they said to him and to the other apostles, 'Brothers, what should we do?'

Peter replied, 'Each of you must repent of your sins and turn to God, and be baptized in the name of Jesus Christ for the forgiveness of your sins. Then you will receive the gift of the Holy Spirit. This promise is to you, to your children, and to those far away—all who have been called by the Lord our God.' Then Peter continued preaching for a long time, strongly urging all his listeners, 'Save yourselves from this crooked generation!'

Those who believed what Peter said were baptized and added to the church that day—about 3,000 in all.

Discussion Starters

1. Why was it necessary for Jesus to ascend to the Father for the Holy Spirit to be released?

_____

_____

_____

_____

_____

2. What is the significance of the gift of tongues?

_____

_____

_____

_____

_____

3. What does it mean to be filled with the Holy Spirit if the Holy Spirit lives inside us?

_____

_____

_____

_____

_____

4. Why do some consider the baptism in the Holy Spirit and the gift of tongues to be so controversial?

_____

_____

_____

_____

_____

5. What is the difference between a dream and a vision?

_____

_____

_____

_____

_____

6. What is the significance of quoting the prophet Joel and quoting David from Psalm 16 in Acts 2?

_____

_____

_____

_____

_____

7. What does the Holy Spirit enable us to do?

_____

_____

_____

_____

_____

8. How have you seen the power of the Holy Spirit at work in your life or the ministry of others?

_____

_____

_____

_____

_____

Final Thoughts

In the previous study on Jesus in the wilderness, we saw how the Holy Spirit led Jesus to victory over the devil. The Holy Spirit is the source of Jesus' power, which is the same power given to the Early Church to fulfil Jesus' mission. It is also given to enable us to '*Go into all the world and preach the gospel to all creation*' (Mark 16:15). It's incredible to think that we have the 24/7 resurrected power of Jesus available to us through the Holy Spirit.

When we are filled with the Holy Spirit it's like having our own Pentecost – we are empowered by the resurrection power of Jesus, enabling us to minister as He did. It's like plugging a mobile phone into an electricity source; we are supercharged by the Holy Spirit to do '*great exploits*' (Dan. 11:32, NKJV). Jesus talks about receiving the Holy Spirit as a 'drink' (John 7:38, NLT), but Paul also reminds us that we need to 'ever be filled' with the Holy Spirit (Eph. 5:18, Amplified).

The New Testament is the fulfilment of Old Testament predictions. Joel's prediction, mentioned in Acts 2, is fulfilled in Jesus: 'In the last days … I will pour out my Spirit on all people' (Acts 2:17). Pentecost ushers in a new era of the Spirit.

Closing Prayer

Lord, strengthen us through Your Holy Spirit, so that we, like the Early Church, might be fully equipped and empowered to proclaim the gospel with power and wisdom. Amen.

Imaginative Meditation

The following imaginative meditation is voiced over music on track four, *Empowered by the Holy Spirit*, of the CD *Transformed by the Holy Spirit*. Available from **www.lizbabbs.com**

Imagine yourself in the upper room with the disciples, just enjoying their company.

What might you ask them?

And now become aware of God's presence with you.

How are you feeling?

What do you see?

What can you hear?

And now become aware of a sound like a violent wind filling the room … and a powerful, fire-like force coming to rest on you.

What is your reaction?

What do you feel?

What is happening now?

> 'In the last days,' God says, 'I will pour out my Spirit upon all people. Your sons and daughters will prophesy. Your young men will see visions, and your old men will dream dreams. In those days I will pour out my Spirit even on my servants—men and women alike—and they will prophesy. And I will cause wonders in the heavens above and signs on the earth below—blood and fire and clouds of smoke. The sun will become dark, and the moon will turn blood red before that great and glorious day of the LORD arrives. But everyone who calls on the name of the LORD will be saved.'
> (Acts 2:17–21, NLT)

Space to Journal

_____
_____
_____
_____
_____
_____
_____
_____
_____
_____
_____
_____
_____
_____
_____
_____
_____
_____
_____
_____
_____
_____
_____
_____
_____
_____
_____
_____
_____
_____

Transformed by the Holy Spirit

Acts 9:1–19

Thought Starter

Ask the person opposite you to hold up their Bible (or this book) at a distance to see if you can read it. How clearly can you see the words?

If you're studying this independently, you might like to place your Bible at a distance to see if you can read it and journal how challenging it is to read the words.

Opening Prayer

Lord of all transformation, continue to mould and refine us so that we reflect Your glory. Amen.

Bible Readings

Luke 15:7
I tell you that in the same way there will be more rejoicing in heaven over one sinner who repents than over ninety-nine righteous people who do not need to repent.

Romans 12:2
Do not conform to the pattern of this world, but be transformed by the renewing of your mind. Then you will be able to test and approve what God's will is – his good, pleasing and perfect will.

Acts 1:8
But you will receive power when the Holy Spirit comes on you; and you will be my witnesses in Jerusalem, and in all Judea and Samaria, and to the ends of the earth.

1 Corinthians 6:19–20
Do you not know that your bodies are temples of the Holy Spirit, who is in you, whom you have received from God? You are not your own; you were bought at a price. Therefore honour God with your bodies.

The Great Commission – Matthew 28:16–20
Then the eleven disciples went to Galilee, to the mountain where Jesus had told them to go. When they saw him, they worshipped him; but some doubted.

Then Jesus came to them and said, 'All authority in heaven and on earth has been given to me. Therefore go and make disciples of all nations, baptising them in the name of the Father and of the Son and of the Holy Spirit, and teaching them to obey everything I have commanded you. And surely I am with you always, to the very end of the age.'

1 Thessalonians 1:4–6

For we know, brothers and sisters loved by God, that he has chosen you, because our gospel came to you not simply with words but also with power, with the Holy Spirit and deep conviction. You know how we lived among you for your sake. You became imitators of us and of the Lord, for you welcomed the message in the midst of severe suffering with the joy given by the Holy Spirit.

Eye Opener

Like many people over a certain age, I need reading glasses to see text clearly. I'm not prepared to wear my glasses on a cord, so my reading glasses also double as a hairband so I don't lose them. My optician does not approve of this practice as it bends the frame. Another problem is seeing through them as I usually forget to clean them. But boy, when I do I see so much more clearly. It's amazing. The world looks different through clean glasses!

Setting the Scene

Saul of Tarsus was born a Jew, but because his father was a Roman citizen, he also had the Latin name Paul. He grew up in a strict Pharisee environment where the name Saul would have been appropriate, but after his conversion he used his Latin name Paul as this was a name the Gentiles would be more familiar with and would aid his mission.

Saul was famous for persecuting Christians and approving Stephen's execution (Acts 8:1). But it was as Paul was travelling from Jerusalem to Syrian Damascus, to imprison

the disciples of Jesus, that he was struck down by a blinding light and experienced a life-changing encounter with the risen Lord. His blindness lasted for three days and it was during that time that a radical transformation took place, one that would have a global impact. His eyes were opened to the truth of the gospel.

Saul was blinded for a purpose and had his own wilderness experience forcing him to do battle with himself and the devil. But he began his journey of healing when he saw the light and recognised Jesus. Even today having a 'Damascus Road' experience is used metaphorically for anyone who has had a sudden change of thought or radical change of direction.

Session Focus

Relax, close your eyes and imagine yourself on the road to Damascus with Saul.

As you listen to this passage of Scripture read to you, see if any words or sentences stand out or become highlighted for you in some way. At the end of the reading, spend a couple of minutes in silence; asking God to show you what He might be saying to you through any words, thoughts or images that drop into your mind. Then discuss your thoughts with your group.

Alternatively, if you are studying this book independently, why not listen to the passage using a Bible audio recording and write your thoughts down in a journal.

Saul's Conversion (Acts 9:1-19)

Meanwhile, Saul was still breathing out murderous threats against the Lord's disciples. He went to the high priest and asked him for letters to the synagogues in Damascus, so that if he found any there who belonged to the Way, whether men or women, he might take them as prisoners to Jerusalem. As he neared Damascus on his journey, suddenly a light from heaven flashed around him. He fell to the ground and heard a voice say to him, 'Saul, Saul, why do you persecute me?'

'Who are you, Lord?' Saul asked.

'I am Jesus, whom you are persecuting,' he replied.

'Now get up and go into the city, and you will be told what you must do.'

The men travelling with Saul stood there speechless; they heard the sound but did not see anyone. Saul got up from the ground, but when he opened his eyes he could see nothing. So they led him by the hand into Damascus. For three days he was blind, and did not eat or drink anything.

In Damascus there was a disciple named Ananias. The Lord called to him in a vision, 'Ananias!'

'Yes, Lord,' he answered.

The Lord told him, 'Go to the house of Judas on Straight Street and ask for a man from Tarsus named Saul, for he is praying. In a vision he has seen a man named Ananias come and place his hands on him to restore his sight.'

'Lord,' Ananias answered, 'I have heard many reports about this man and all the harm he has done to your holy people in Jerusalem. And he has come here with authority from the chief priests to arrest all who call on your name.'

But the Lord said to Ananias, 'Go! This man is my chosen instrument to proclaim my name to the Gentiles and their kings and to the people of Israel. I will show him how much he must suffer for my name.'

Then Ananias went to the house and entered it. Placing his hands on Saul, he said, 'Brother Saul, the Lord – Jesus, who appeared to you on the road as you were coming here – has sent me so that you may see again and be filled with the Holy Spirit.' Immediately, something like scales fell from Saul's eyes, and he could see again. He got up and was baptised, and after taking some food, he regained his strength.

Discussion Starters

1. Why was Saul murdering Christians?

_____

_____

_____

_____

_____

2. What is the light that Saul sees?

_____

_____

_____

_____

_____

3. Why was it necessary to blind Saul?

_____

_____

_____

_____

_____

4. What is a vision?

_____

_____

_____

_____

_____

5. Have you ever had a vision or dream? If so, share it with the group or journal it if you're studying this alone.

_____

_____

_____

_____

_____

6. Why didn't Jesus heal Saul directly? What might have happened if Ananias had been too scared to pray for Saul?

_____

_____

_____

_____

_____

7. What might the 'scales' be that fell off Saul's eyes?

_____

_____

_____

_____

_____

8. Are there any ways in which Saul's story echoes your spiritual journey?

_____

_____

_____

_____

_____

Final Thoughts

The life of Saul/Paul demonstrates that our failures don't have to define us; in fact they can qualify us for service. Who would have thought that one of the greatest heroes of Christianity would be someone who persecuted Christians.

Paul was a church planter and world changer who dictated many letters to the churches under the inspiration of the Holy Spirit. Without him we'd lose half of the New Testament, such is the significance of his ministry and writing. What an incredible legacy.

It's interesting to reflect on how differently things might have turned out if Ananias had listened to his fears and not obeyed God. Despite his initial reluctance, Ananias prayed for Saul and the Holy Spirit was released so powerfully through him that

Saul could see clearly both physically and spiritually, and was then baptised. Saul's conversion is like a modern-day terrorist becoming the most powerful Christian leader in history.

Closing Prayer

Lord Jesus, transform and empower us through Your Spirit and fill us with Your resurrection joy so that it spills over to others. Amen.

Imaginative Meditation

The following imaginative meditation is voiced over music on track five, *Transformed by the Holy Spirit*, of the CD *Transformed by the Holy Spirit*. Available from **www.lizbabbs.com**

Turn off any lights, close your eyes and sit in the dark for a few minutes, just enjoying God's presence.

Now, as you open your eyes, allowing them time to adjust to the light, imagine Jesus is in the room with you.

What can you see?

What are you feeling?

Where is Jesus in the room?

Is Jesus saying anything to you?

What's your response?

What is Jesus doing?

Do you sense Jesus showing you anything?

Now allow the Holy Spirit to fill you as you breathe in God's presence.

Space to Journal

_____
_____
_____
_____
_____
_____
_____
_____
_____
_____
_____
_____
_____
_____
_____
_____
_____
_____
_____
_____
_____
_____
_____
_____
_____
_____
_____
_____
_____
_____
_____
_____
_____

Revealed by the Holy Spirit
Revelation 1:1-20

Thought Starter

Ask one person in the group to read aloud a paragraph from Revelation 1 as fast as they can, and the rest of the group to write it down. Now see how much of the text group members can read back from their notes. If you're studying this independently, try writing down a paragraph with your non-dominant hand. How much can you read?

Opening Prayer

Lord, reveal Yourself to us as You did John, and increase our understanding of Your plan for this world and the next. Amen.

Bible Readings

The Judgment of the Dead – Revelation 20:11–15

Then I saw a great white throne and him who was seated on it. The earth and the heavens fled from his presence, and there was no place for them. And I saw the dead, great and small, standing before the throne, and books were opened. Another book was opened, which is the book of life. The dead were judged according to what they had done as recorded in the books. The sea gave up the dead that were in it, and death and Hades gave up the dead that were in them, and each person was judged according to what they had done. Then death and Hades were thrown into the lake of fire. The lake of fire is the second death. Anyone whose name was not found written in the book of life was thrown into the lake of fire.

A New Heaven and a New Earth – Revelation 21:1–4

Then I saw 'a new heaven and a new earth,' for the first heaven and the first earth had passed away, and there was no longer any sea. I saw the Holy City, the new Jerusalem, coming down out of heaven from God, prepared as a bride beautifully dressed for her husband. And I heard a loud voice from the throne saying, 'Look! God's dwelling-place is now among the people, and he will dwell with them.

They will be his people, and God himself will be with them and be their God. "He will wipe every tear from their eyes. There will be no more death" or mourning or crying or pain, for the old order of things has passed away.'

The New Jerusalem, the Bride of the Lamb – Revelation 21:9–14

One of the seven angels who had the seven bowls full of the seven last plagues came and said to me, 'Come, I will show you the bride, the wife of the Lamb.' And he carried me away in the Spirit to a mountain great and high, and showed me the Holy City, Jerusalem, coming down out of heaven from God. It shone with the glory of God, and its brilliance was like that of a very precious jewel, like a jasper, clear as crystal. It had a great, high wall with twelve gates, and with twelve angels at the gates. On the gates were written the names of the twelve tribes of Israel. There were three gates on the east, three on the north, three on the south and three on the west. The wall of the city had twelve foundations, and on them were the names of the twelve apostles of the Lamb.

Eden Restored – Revelation 22:1–5,17

Then the angel showed me the river of the water of life, as clear as crystal, flowing from the throne of God and of the Lamb down the middle of the great street of the city. On each side of the river stood the tree of life, bearing twelve crops of fruit, yielding its fruit every month. And the leaves of the tree are for the healing of the nations. No longer will there be any curse. The throne of God and of the Lamb will be in the city, and his servants will serve him. They will see his face, and his name will be on their foreheads. There will be no more night. They will not need the light of a lamp or the light of the sun, for the Lord God will give them light. And they will reign for ever and ever ... The Spirit and the bride say, 'Come!' And let the one who hears say, 'Come!' Let the one who is thirsty come; and let the one who wishes take the free gift of the water of life.

Eye Opener

This is my fourteenth published book, and the writing process for nearly every one of my books is different. This book has required me to go away at regular intervals to a hotel so that God could reveal, through the Holy Spirit, what should be included in each study. This is a completely different work pattern to any of my other books. In practical terms it made little sense as it took at least eighty minutes to drive to a destination where I wouldn't be distracted and hotels aren't cheap. However, as I've spent time reflecting on the Bible study passages in this book, especially Exodus 31 and Revelation 1, I realised what a privileged position I was in – God had chosen me to write this book on the Holy Spirit and set me aside on a 'desert island' just off the M62! The hotel chain really looked after me, allocating me a quiet room away from everyone, and allowed me late checkout so I could maximise my time there. They even looked after my NIV Study Bible when I left it there between visits. Towards the end of my stay they awarded me VIP status, something which has never happened to me before. But this reminded me that, to God, we are VIPs – very important people doing a very important job that He has revealed to us; gifted and equipped us to do.

Setting the Scene

To God, John was a VIP, a prophet set aside on the island of Patmos, commissioned to write down the revelation of Jesus Christ through the Holy Spirit. John, who some believe was John the apostle, was effectively taking dictation – writing down the messages Jesus gave him for the seven churches!

The Greek word for revelation is *apokalupsis*, which means 'apocalypse' or 'revealing' or 'unveiling'. Revelation is a book for the Church that includes predictive prophesy showing what will happen in the future. The visions lay out God's timetable for the future history of the world. The main message is that despite the apparent mess the world is in, God is still King and Jesus Christ

is returning in triumph and will rule with authority; setting up a new heaven and new earth.

John is given mind-blowing visions from heaven that he expresses in his own language. But it's very hard to express anything visual or symbolic in writing. Words are limited and John is trying to describe the indescribable, which is why Revelation can seem a rather strange off-putting book to read.

Session Focus

Relax, close your eyes and imagine yourself like John, commissioned and ready to take dictation from Jesus.

As you listen to this passage of Scripture read to you, see if any words or sentences stand out or become highlighted for you in some way. At the end of the reading, spend a couple of minutes in silence; asking God to show you what He might be saying to you through any words, thoughts or images that drop into your mind. Then discuss your thoughts with your group.

Alternatively, if you are studying this book independently, why not listen to the passage using a Bible audio recording and write your thoughts down in a journal.

Revelation 1:1–20

The revelation from Jesus Christ, which God gave him to show his servants what must soon take place. He made it known by sending his angel to his servant John, who testifies to everything he saw – that is, the word of God and the testimony of Jesus Christ. Blessed is the one who reads aloud the words of this prophecy, and blessed are those who hear it and take to heart what is written in it, because the time is near.

John,

To the seven churches in the province of Asia:

Grace and peace to you from him who is, and who was, and who is to come, and from the seven spirits before his throne, and from Jesus Christ, who is the faithful witness, the firstborn from the dead, and the ruler of the kings of the earth.

To him who loves us and has freed us from our sins by his blood, and has made us to be a kingdom and priests to serve his God and Father – to him be glory and power for ever and ever! Amen.

'Look, he is coming with the clouds,'
and 'every eye will see him,
even those who pierced him';
and all peoples on earth 'will mourn because of him.'
So shall it be! Amen.

'I am the Alpha and the Omega,' says the Lord God, 'who is, and who was, and who is to come, the Almighty.'

I, John, your brother and companion in the suffering and kingdom and patient endurance that are ours in Jesus, was on the island of Patmos because of the word of God and the testimony of Jesus. On the Lord's Day I was in the Spirit, and I heard behind me a loud voice like a trumpet, which said: 'Write on a scroll what you see and send it to the seven churches: to Ephesus, Smyrna, Pergamum, Thyatira, Sardis, Philadelphia and Laodicea.'

I turned round to see the voice that was speaking to me. And when I turned I saw seven golden lampstands, and among the lampstands was someone like a son of man, dressed in a robe reaching down to his feet and with a golden sash round his chest. The hair on his head was white like wool, as white as snow, and his eyes were like blazing fire. His feet were like bronze glowing in a furnace, and his voice was like the sound of rushing waters. In his right hand he held seven stars, and coming out of his mouth was a sharp, double-edged sword. His face was like the sun shining in all its brilliance.

When I saw him, I fell at his feet as though dead. Then he placed his right hand on me and said: 'Do not be afraid. I am the First and the Last. I am the Living One; I was dead, and now look, I am alive for ever and ever! And I hold the keys of death and Hades.

'Write, therefore, what you have seen, what is now and what will take place later. The mystery of the seven stars that you saw in my right hand and of the seven golden lampstands is this: the seven stars are the angels of the seven churches, and the seven lampstands are the seven churches.

Discussion Starters

1. What is a prophetic vision?

_____

_____

_____

_____

_____

2. What does John mean by saying he was 'in the Spirit' (Rev. 1:10)?

_____

_____

_____

_____

_____

3. What do you understand about angels?

_____

_____

_____

_____

_____

4. What is meant when the Lord God says 'I am the Alpha and the Omega ... who is, and who was, and who is to come, the Almighty' (Rev. 1:8)?

_____

_____

_____

_____

_____

5. What is the sharp double-edged sword?

_____
_____
_____
_____
_____

6. When John said these things will shortly take place,
   what did he mean?

_____
_____
_____
_____
_____

7. Is this message meant just for the seven churches or is it
   relevant for us today?

_____
_____
_____
_____
_____

8. What would be your reaction if God asked you to take down
   dictation about Himself?

_____
_____
_____
_____
_____
_____

Final Thoughts

When John saw Jesus, it's hardly surprising he fell on his face. And yet we see Jesus' love and care for John in that despite the enormity of what Jesus was about to share, He had time for him, offering him reassurance by placing His right hand on him. This is the personal face of God.

No other New Testament book is more difficult to understand and more open to different interpretations than Revelation. Many people avoid reading this book for that reason, but when we understand how things end, the whole Bible makes sense. To study the Bible without reading Revelation is like abandoning a book partway through or walking out of a gripping movie without seeing the end. Genesis and Revelation are the two bookends of the Bible, holding everything together. In the book of Revelation, the devil is defeated and thrown into a lake of burning sulphur (Rev. 20:10), we see the curse removed, creation restored and access to the tree of life again (Rev. 22:2–3). The end – the restoration, makes sense of the beginning – the Fall, and all that follows. In addition, we are told that we will even see God's face (Rev. 22:4).

Revelation is inspirational. It's incredible to think that just by reading aloud or listening to Revelation and internalising it, we are blessed (Rev. 1:3). I believe if we read it as frequently as we do the Psalms, it would feed our faith and fuel our sense of mission.

Closing Prayer

Lord, we're amazed and awestruck by Your eternal plans, which are revealed through Your Word. Help us to live and walk in the assurance of Your victory. Amen.

Imaginative Meditation

The following imaginative meditation is voiced over music on track six, *Revealed by the Holy Spirit*, of the CD *Transformed by the Holy Spirit*. Available from **www.lizbabbs.com**

Imagine you've been commissioned, like John in Revelation, to write down whatever God dictates.

Now pray and ask the Holy Spirit to reveal something about Jesus to you.

Now imagine yourself holding a pen and writing this revelation down on paper.

What are you writing?

What is Jesus sharing with you?

What is your response?

What happens next?

Now imagine yourself reading this revelation to others.

Space to Journal

_____
_____
_____
_____
_____
_____
_____
_____
_____
_____
_____
_____
_____
_____
_____
_____
_____
_____
_____
_____
_____
_____
_____
_____
_____
_____
_____
_____
_____
_____
_____
_____
_____
_____

Leader's Notes

General Notes on Leading the Studies

The aim of the six studies in this book is to help people gain an increased awareness of the activity of the Holy Spirit from creation to Revelation and consequently a deeper understanding of the nature of the triune God. The approach I've taken is both interactive and reflective, encouraging individuals to understand Scripture from the inside out.

This book has been designed so that it can be used like a journal to record notes and reflections, and so I have included 'Space to Journal' sections. Consequently, it would be beneficial if everyone in a group had their own copy.

Members of the group might like to reflect on a scripture a day from the Bible Readings section to increase their knowledge of key passages about the Holy Spirit.

I recommend using the Imaginative Meditations I've voiced over music from the *Transformed by the Holy Spirit* CD (or MP3 download). This could also be used in between sessions as a personal meditation by individuals in the group.

I have written each Session Focus section in the studies so that it can be approached reflectively. This allows individuals and members of the group to step inside the passage of Scripture and encourages a heart response, not just a head response. It also gives the group the opportunity to engage with the passage experientially before more traditional Bible discussion questions might be used afterwards. Questions may well arise out of this time of reflection too, but this approach initiates a response from group members, which is very valuable in the learning process.

At the beginning of each Session Focus I have written a short introduction:

Relax, close your eyes and imagine ... As you listen to this passage of Scripture read to you several times, see if any words or sentences stand out or become highlighted in some way. At the end of the readings, spend a couple of minutes in silence; asking God to show you what He might be saying to

you through any words, thoughts or images that drop into your mind. Then discuss your thoughts with your group or take time to record them for your own personal reflection.

How to Lead the Session Focus Reflectively

Here are some ideas to help you as you lead these sections of the book:

1. I project visuals, which are often works of art or photographs, to help open up the passage of Scripture to those who are more visual learners like myself. These images are readily available using the Internet. Many by artist and illustrator Harold Copping are suitable.

2. In addition to recording the CD *Transformed by the Holy Spirit*, which has the six Imaginative Meditations in this book voiced over music, my concert album *Ruach – Spirit of God*, contains Bible readings from this book and additional tracks, which would create a powerful backdrop and addition to this book. You might like to introduce or complete this book by inviting musician Simeon Wood and myself to perform *Ruach* in concert at your church or local venue. *Ruach* is a celebration of the Holy Spirit using the arts.

3. At the beginning of each Session Focus you could pray, 'Lord, we ask that You would speak to us through Your Word and like Samuel we pray, "Speak, for your servant is listening" (1 Sam. 3:10).'

4. It is best if group members don't look up the passage for the first reading. Encourage them to relax, put their books and pens down and close their eyes as you read the passage slowly to them. Then ask them to see if any words, thoughts, images or sentences stand out from the passage (as though they were highlighted by a marker pen).

5. At the end of the first reading give them a few minutes to reflect in silence and to ask God to show them how He might be speaking to them through their highlighted word or words.

6. Then read the passage through slowly again, or use a Bible audio recording such as David Suchet's reading from the NIV (Hodder & Stoughton) or for a more dramatised reading:

The Bible Experience (Zondervan). If individuals want to follow the passage this time, they can, but it is not necessary. (They are welcome to look anything up at the end of this second reading.)
7. Having read the passage aloud twice to the group, give them a few minutes again to reflect on their personal highlighted word and what God might be saying to them. (If you are short of time, you could just read the passage once instead of twice, especially if it's a long passage, but it is best to read it twice.)
8. Then invite them to share their thoughts, highlighted words or questions with the group. To encourage this personal sharing, explain that sharing thoughts and ideas with the group can help others who feel they've not received anything specific. It is also important that there is no pressure to share or to share more personally than a person might wish.

Study One: Created by the Holy Spirit

Thought Starter
It's important to begin the description of making a cup of tea using the words 'In the beginning' because it encourages people to be more creative in their thinking and leads to some interesting statements.

Imaginative Meditation
This particular imaginative meditation comes before the Session Focus as it prepares groups and individuals for what, very importantly, is to be studied further: that the Holy Spirit was present right at the beginning of creation. I greatly encourage groups and individuals to watch the video 'Spirit of Creation' on my YouTube channel. The audio version is also available as track one, *Created by the Holy Spirit*, of the CD *Transformed by the Holy Spirit*. Available from **www.lizbabbs.com**

Study Four: Empowered by the Holy Spirit

You might like to anoint each other's hands with oil at some point during this session, as a symbol of wanting to receive more of the Holy Spirit.

Study Six: Revealed by the Holy Spirit

Bible Readings

I've included four key passages from Revelation to provide a context and snapshot overview of the book of Revelation, so the group can see where Revelation fits in with the rest of the Bible. It would be helpful to spend some time reflecting upon these passages, in addition to the Session Focus of Revelation 1.

Setting the Scene

It's important to demystify the book of Revelation as much as possible, as many people have reservations about it and might fear tackling it. Some might only be aware of the demonic references in Revelation through watching horror movies and so it is important to listen to everyone's anxieties and misconceptions early on in this session and to set the record straight by offering a biblical framework to understand this book.

Free Additional Resources

For video meditations and interviews with Liz Babbs, visit her YouTube channel at **www.youtube.com/lizbabbs**

OTHER

Liz Babbs

TITLES

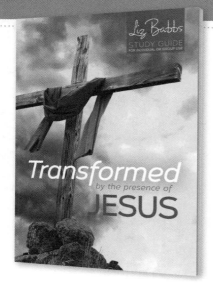

Transformed by the Presence of Jesus

Over six studies, Liz invites us to adopt a meditative approach to reading Scripture. Go beyond traditional Bible study and step into the shoes of many well-known Bible characters, all of whom were transformed by their encounters with Jesus.

Ideal for individual or group use.
ISBN: 978-1-78259-237-2

Transformed by Love

Divided into twelve different themes, this special book of prayers and reflections seeks both to encourage readers to talk honestly with God, and also deepen their understanding of God's unconditional and transforming love.

ISBN: 978-1-78259-262-4

For current prices visit **www.cwr.org.uk/store**
Available online or from Christian bookshops.

Courses and seminars

Waverley Abbey College

Publishing and media

Conference facilities

Transforming lives

CWR's vision is to enable people to experience personal transformation through applying God's Word to their lives and relationships.

Our Bible-based training and resources help people around the world to:
• Grow in their walk with God
• Understand and apply Scripture to their lives
• Resource themselves and their church
• Develop pastoral care and counselling skills
• Train for leadership
• Strengthen relationships, marriage and family life and much more.

Our insightful writers provide daily Bible reading notes and other resources for all ages, and our experienced course designers and presenters have gained an international reputation for excellence and effectiveness.

CWR's Training and Conference Centres in Surrey and East Sussex, England, provide excellent facilities in idyllic settings – ideal for both learning and spiritual refreshment.

CWR Applying God's Word
to everyday life and relationships

CWR, Waverley Abbey House,
Waverley Lane, Farnham,
Surrey GU9 8EP, UK

Telephone: **+44 (0)1252 784700**
Email: info@cwr.org.uk
Website: www.cwr.org.uk

Registered Charity No. 294387
Company Registration No. 1990308